Magical Mother Goose

MW01629172

Adapted by John Archambault & David Plummer

Illustrated by Robert Sauber

Childcraft Education Corp.

Text Copyright © 2006
John Archambault
&
David Plummer

Illustrations Copyright © 2006
Robert Sauber

All rights reserved

Childcraft Education Corp.
1156 Four Star Drive
Mount Joy, PA 17552

A Member of the School Speciality® Family

Printed in China

ISBN 1-58669-188-0

There Was a Little Girl is commonly believed to be a Mother Goose Rhyme. However, this rhyme was written by poet Henry Wadsworth Longfellow (February 27, 1807 – March 24, 1882). It's believed Longfellow wrote this poem about his daughter.

For Daniel Jacob, my new nephew–
sing and read with me

JA

To Nancy Lee who believes in me

DP

To the most magical of spirits,
my daughter, Sophie

RS

There Was a Little Girl

There was a little girl, who had a little curl,
Right in the middle of her forehead.
When she was good,
She was very, very good.
And when she was bad, she was horrid.

There was a little girl, who had a little curl,
Right in the middle of her forehead.
And when she was good,
She was very, very good.
And when she was bad, she was horrid.

And when she was bad, she was horrid.

Little Robin Redbreast

Little Robin Redbreast sat upon a tree.
Up went Pussycat, and down went he!
Down came Pussycat, and away Robin ran.
Said Little Robin Redbreast,
"Catch me if you can!"

Little Robin Redbreast jumped upon a wall.
Pussycat jumped up to him,
And almost had a fall.
Little Robin Redbreast chirped
"How do you do?"
Pussycat said "Meow,"
and away Robin flew.

This is the way we go to school

This is the way we go to school,
Go to school, go to school.
This is the way we go to school,
On a cold and frosty morning.

This is the way we come out of school,
Come out of school, come out of school.
This is the way we come out of school,
On a cold and frosty morning.

RSauber

Jack and Jill

Jack and Jill went up the hill
To fetch a pail of water.
Jack fell down and broke his crown.
And Jill came tumbling after.

Jack and Jill went up the hill
To fetch a pail of water.
Jack fell down and broke his crown.
And Jill came tumbling after.

R.Sauber

Mother Goose
R. Sauber